Waking Stone

ALSO BY CAROLE SIMMONS OLES

The Loneliness Factor

Quarry

Night Watches:
Inventions on the Life of Maria Mitchell

Stunts

The Deed

Sympathetic Systems

Greatest Hits (1979–2005)

WAKING STONE

Inventions on the Life of Harriet Hosmer

BY CAROLE SIMMONS OLES

The University of Arkansas Press
Fayetteville
2006

⊗ The paper used in this publication meets the minimum
requirements of the American National Standard for Permanence
of Paper for Printed Library Materials Z39.48-1984.

LIBRARY OF CONGRESS CATALOGING-IN-PUBLICATION DATA

Oles, Carole.
Waking stone : inventions on the life of Harriet Hosmer /
by Carole Simmons Oles.
p.   cm.
ISBN 1-55728-825-9 (alk. paper)
1. Hosmer, Harriet Goodhue, 1830–1908—Poetry. I. Title.
PS3565.L43W35   2006
811'.54—dc22
2006011828

To Max

ACKNOWLEDGMENTS

Poems from this manuscript have appeared in the following publications, sometimes in different form:

Alaska Quarterly: "Zenobia Speaks, in Chains and Free," "Thinking, Making Ready"; *The Alaska Review:* "Beginning and Ending with Mahler's *Kindertotenlieder*"; *Greatest Hits:* "Astoria, New York Interlude: Italian Notebook"; *Hayden's Ferry Review:* "Mother at Her Easel: A Memory," "Purification"; *Introspections: American Poets on One of Their Own Poems:* "Her Story: My Daughter Beatrice"; *The Journal:* "The Body Forbidden," "On Marriage, How Many Times Must I Tell You," and "Rumor"; *Night Watches:* "Astronomer Maria Mitchell Meets Harriet Hosmer" (under the title "Harriet Hosmer of Watertown, Massachusetts"); *The Onset Review:* "Crossing Zones," "I Find My Place: Mrs. Sedgwick's School," and "I Misbehave: Self-Defenses"; *Painted Bride Quarterly:* "Parallel Universes"; *Prairie Schooner:* "The Critics Comment on *Zenobia*," "February 21, Then and Now," "Finding My Master," "Hatty to Posterity," "I Fight the Battle of the Amazons," "I Rededicate Watertown's Hosmer School to You, Hatty," "I Tell Hatty the Effacing Dream," "Making Money," "Preparing for Dinner Guests, Mindful of Hatty," "To Hatty on Easter Sunday, Among Spirits," and "Tomb of Judith Falconnet"; *Quarry:* "Stonecarver, Restoring"; *The Women's Review of Books:* "My Clothes," "My First Child, and Another Daughter."

I am deeply grateful to The Schlesinger Library at Radcliffe Institute for Advanced Study for use of its extensive resources, many of which have influenced these poems. Thanks to The Schlesinger Library staff for its generosity and eagerness to assist in every possible way. My gratitude also to Watertown Public Library for access to its Hosmer archives and for the aid of its staff.

Thanks to the American Academy in Rome and The MacDowell Colony for residencies during which some of these poems were written.

CONTENTS

FOREWORD

These poems are based on the life of American sculptor Harriet Hosmer (1830-1908), born in Watertown, Massachusetts, and raised by her physician father after her mother died of consumption when Hatty was four. The family also lost three children to the disease; reference is made to these deaths in some of the poems. Hatty was a notoriously wild child who from an early age resolved to be a sculptor. At twenty-two, she left for Rome to study and stayed in Europe for some forty years. At first apprenticed to English sculptor John Gibson, Hosmer eventually opened her own studio. Some of her works or copies of them are seen today in the Boston Museum of Fine Arts, the Wadsworth Atheneum, and Wellesley College, among other locations. Many of her works have disappeared. While in Rome, Hosmer eventually led a group of women sculptors called by Henry James "The White Marmorean Flock"— though the term did not acknowledge the one African/Chippewa American among them, Edmonia Lewis.

I first encountered Harriet Hosmer when I was researching a book based on the life and work of astronomer Maria Mitchell. For many reasons, including my father's stonecarving and my loss of a sibling at an early age, I felt the pull of Hosmer's parallel universe, which led to this dialogue— poems sometimes in her voice, sometimes in mine.

Harriet Hosmer, circa 1860. *Photograph courtesy of The Schlesinger Library, Radcliffe Institute, Harvard University.*

Waking Stone

Invocation to Hatty

Lady of beetles, bugs, stuffed birds in nests
lady of frogs and rats

come to the snakeskin from the shores of Quabbin
the monarch from Virginia, swallowtail from Vermont
come to the brown-paper beetle set with onyx headlamps
and the gauze biplane that pulses on my mantel
come to the armored horseshoe crab, the tracery of cod
the mermaid's purse with four drawstrings
the tail feather of a turkey that fed in orchards
wing feather of a pheasant that nested in brush

come through these familiars, Hatty
visit these altars, remainders—then show me

what skins you've left behind

Mother at Her Easel: A Memory

I am four, my hand failing to catch hers as it flies
dipping from paints to paper faster than she kneads bread.
The red ball fades and grows, her eyes far from me
when I reach to her face, draw back
as if I've touched the woodstove, mother's cheek
more red than the sunset she streaks across paper.

Years later I will search under eaves for this
painting, this last warm mother . . .

Ice stills the Charles, but when I make worlds
they will contain so little water
they can stand alone, heavier than a mother or sister
stand cool and white, unfevered. Calm.
Find them even now
at the library, in the public square: in Boston, St. Louis,

one at rest in Rome, bright city where I'll learn
just how faithfully stones must obey me.

I Misbehave: Self-Defenses

1840–1845

1.

I have to shoot the robin to take it apart
to study its bones and attachments,
make it calm and still. I have to keep
it from flying, the feathers spread, the cunning
all held by pins for me to get it right.
Father gives me bow and arrow, ivory gun
with a silver nose. I learn to use them.
By the river, in the yard I mix clay
and mold it, my models the worthies
my neighbors won't touch:
frog, snake, rat. *Am* I strange? eccentric?
I am a girl who won't be ground down.
I shape the ground.

2.

To you, Schoolmaster Tedium (*Peabody*)
who never could entrap me
in your tight desks and canon,
I recommend a book I've read of late:
whose heroine, like me, has a message
writ on her back—do you recall sending me
home to Father with a list of my crimes

pinned behind me?—she is called
    Woman Warrior
if you, Mr. P., take my meaning.

3.

All right, so it was dangerous.
I like danger, always. I take the reins.
Yes I ride standing on my horse.
Dared, I ride alone all night to Boston.
Why wait, knitting, for danger to arrive?
Though a girl, I want to engineer.
How droll to uncouple the train—
engine chugging toward Boston
while the passenger cars, gaping, stay home.
When I'm caught with my hand on the links
Father pays damages.
I almost got away with it.
Which of you told?

4.

I confess I killed the Doctor. Well, "killed."
Eliakim Morse looking like Scrooge in his dressing gown,
white stringy hair crawling from his velvet cap.
All he has left is money, for which the town
parts, a Red Sea. Eliakim Morse in his yellow carriage,
more years upon him than the *four*—
mother, sister, two brothers—we lost.
I take charge of death and send a notice

to the papers, then hide among Dutch elms
to watch mourners call at his house.
This is my last, worst offense,
worse by far than nearly drowning,
What will people say?
Father rides me out of town.

I Find My Place:
Mrs. Sedgwick's School

Lenox, Massachusetts, 1845–1849

All these sisters! and Mrs. Sedgwick wise,
kind mother who understands, assures
my father she's trained wild colts before.
We study Latin, French, and Greek; the suspect
Hygiene. We pace strong bodies on the hills
in every season, hear Mrs. Kemble
each Saturday read Shakespeare.
Her counterfeiting Rosalind cheers me best—
bewooded with Orlando, thanking God
she's not a woman, teasing with "a man
haunts the forest, that abuses our young
plants with carving Rosalind on their barks"
and yet she's Rosalind, so many fathoms deep
in love . . . "like the bay of Portugal."
This Fanny Kemble wades in Richmond Pond
for trout and bream, her shocking pantaloons
great lilypads upon the current.
Fanny teaches me to recite for others' joy,
steers my untamed wit away from mischief,
teaches action bridled by words . . . and still,
sometimes I answer urgency along my legs,
an invitation from the world, such as to scale
the tree four stories high to take a crow's nest.

I sway on tossing limbs; below, my friends
gaze open-mouthed like chicks for worms.
What would have become of me if not
for Mrs. Sedgwick's dear instruction?
My place might have been the Concord stocks,
my face might have hung in a post office—
I the bad fruit shaken from my father
the blight afflicting our chestnut,
I the girl child who couldn't be managed.

I Am Lowered, I Am Raised

Lead mine, Dubuque, Iowa, 1850

You know I am fearless on earth, in air—
so I venture down. The one-person
bucket lowered by pulleys is my chariot,
I climb over the rim, clutch the splintery edge.
Dark, darker, and even the lantern
hung from above cannot mimic day,
which may never salve my eyes again.
I try to stand still at the center
but despite my designs, the bucket rocks—
no cradle, but ship torn by a gale
and I feeble swimmer.
Down, further down, and the light
extinguished now. No lid covers me,
worm in a jar, and I sink
like mother's vessel lowered on ropes,
like our Helen's following after . . . I
too could be lost in insatiable
dark, where the smell
rushing off sharp walls is my own flesh.
This is my Hour of Lead.
These brittle chips scooped from the earth
mark my compact: I vow never
to sentence my body to this cavern
except refined by flames.
Ask no more. Reverse the ropes and bring me home.

The Body Forbidden

How dare I.
  With Father's support.
Hours of play with his office skeleton,
nothing macabre or impure
in such fine engineering.
No pretty cameo ornaments
do I wish to carve, but the whole
human form, complete with its stories.

How dare I.
  With my Lenox sisters and models:
Fanny Kemble acting onstage
or casting for trout,
leaving her tyrant husband.
Maria Mitchell discovering a comet
in 1847, my junior year.
Mrs. Sedgwick teaching us Hygiene,
the regimen of female health.

How dare *I* in defiance of Harvard Medical School *and*
the Boston Medical Society with their concerted Nays!
for men owned knowledge like bodies: slaves, wives, the ill.

I dare
  With Dr. Joseph McDowell, surgeon, director
of Missouri Medical College. When he admits

me to anatomy class I go west
to gaze on bodies Harvard only shows men.
I sit on the hard bench in the amphitheater
five months and not one other student
causes me grief. If he did
Dr. McDowell would disembody him.

That Other River: The Mississippi

1850, setting out with Cornelia

Even called the *Pacific*
our steamboat brings little peace,
every two hours snagged on a shoal.
When Cornelia tires of being arrested
and boards a passing boat home,
I risk scandal, continue alone.
The ivory gun sleeps in my hamper.

The *Whirlwind,* smaller vessel
to which we must transfer
when the *Pacific* refuses to be moved,
passes three more trapped boats,
and a fourth which overtook us
an hour ago, now gone under.
Still, this Mississippi disarms me:

brown water's clay pigment,
levee pedestals where children stand
to watch paddlewheels juggle the river.
Its current insists *onward*
to the city of chicory, Cajun, beignets.
Cornelia's father could never do wrong
and he has slaves in his house . . .

I stay away from the auctions.
In my cabin, I study Myology's muscle man
and draw him stepping up,
saluting the sinewy tide.

More Wildlife Study

Aboard the train to Philadelphia, 1850

Installed beside the glass
I am deep into Lydia's pamphlet
An Appeal in Favor of That Class of Americans Called Africans
when I hear a stir in the aisle,
a man tips his bowler, asking
if the empty seat is empty.
What can I say? My book saves me:
after he settles, the train lurches on
and I plunge into Lydia's words.
More rustling. Squirming. Exaggerated
removal of gloves.
When I look up to glare,
he says I have beautiful eyes.
I feel like Red Riding Hood.
I ignore his remark, aim my two orbs,
like gun barrels, at him.
Book, be my rescue! But he charges on,
now telling of his wife and babies.
Oh base suspicion . . . I am ashamed
for several minutes, until
he praises my "pretty little hand."
What a falsehood! I know then
he is a wolf. How I tremble, so grieved

that a father should be a wolf.
But let me not debase *Canis lupus*.
This "pretty little hand," sir, wields chisel on marble.
This hand itches to box your soft mouth.

Linkage

Tracking you, Hatty
over the brink of the twenty-first century
all roads lead me
to you and your time. For instance

your friend Lydia Maria Child,
most famous American woman author
of her day, and missing from
The Norton Anthology of Literature by Women.
Precursor of Stowe against slavery, writing
An Appeal in Favor of That Class of Americans Called Africans
in 1833.

Now, in northern California,
Black History Month, Cornel West
lamenting slavery's enduring blot,
pays tribute to that Lydia who wrote
        "I am fully aware of the unpopularity of the task
        I have undertaken; but though I *expect*
        ridicule and censure, it is not in my nature to *fear* them."

You, Hatty, so otherwise just
preferred to think all slaveowners
as kind as your Missouri second father
and patron, Wayman Crow.
Lydia teased you

"I can send you a Bowie knife
bearing the motto 'Death
to the Abolitionists,' if you want it,
but Bowie knives won't kill us."
Yet facing one sister sculptor
African/Chippewa Edmonia Lewis
in Rome you served as her mentor and friend.

Last night I dreamed I was a stop
on the underground railway.
Soldiers wearing guns and bloody jackets
massed outside in the dark
to find my charge shivering beside me.
I woke as hate peered in
with long teeth and wide, blazing eyes.
I woke before it could harvest strange fruit.

You hear Cornel West:
how the nation still bleeds, how in all
white supremacy curdles—
the tapeworm feeding on him, on me, on you.

From Backyard Studio, to Rome, 1852

1.

Everything has prepared me for study in Rome
and now the invitation from Miss Cushman
gives me a home with her, Mathilda Hayes,
and Sarah Jane Clarke: prospect sublime.
I work night and day on the *Hesper.*
I think the sad Hesper one of Tennyson's
most exquisite images. Mine I take
from clay to marble, beating my hands to pieces
ten hours a day in the backyard studio,
the grove of elms. A veil of marble dust
covers all—rasp, chisels, mallet,
punch, auger, calipers hung on the wall
like paintings in the Boston Atheneum.
How lucky that Father thinks my art no hobby
but profession. Lucky am I in fathers.
I will never say aloud what weighs on me:
Mother, Helen, the babies Hiram and George.
Beating my hands to beat out from stone
lives indestructible, calm. *Hesper.*
I wish my loved ones such awakenings:
after each night, rising as morning stars.
Star at her crown, moon beneath her breast,
poppy capsules woven in her hair,
my *Hesper*'s eyes are half-closing
to a music just beyond our power to hear.

I have let a workman do but one day's job
chopping the largest corners of the marble
block inside which Hesper dreamed.

2.

On the eve of departure I dream
my return to this place on Riverside Street
the tall white house with green shutters,
Mrs. Coolidge rocking on the balcony
looks up when I call
then I am stretching in our copper tub
a carp at my toes
I am gorging apples from the kitchen bins
then the house is gone
in its place a box of bricks
with identical twin brothers
the Francis house next door to ours
a temporary residence for the dead
my studio nowhere, the elms
that fanned our summers vanished
the Charles coughing up foam
fish drying on the banks
a shudder in the earth
a train on wheels,
lights and buzzers
commerce all bloated

I almost fear to leave

Enroute to Rome, October, 1852

day after day I make the rounds on deck
keeping fit, filling my lungs with balm
to banish the dry cough Father hears
as the echo of Mother's and Helen's
I must believe that soon water will yield
to Obelisk, Coliseum, Piazzas, the din of commerce
the Tiber will couch in humanity's grip

crossing the unbounded ocean
I cease: loosed from earth
not assumed into air
darkness swirls through my thoughts—
the mine shaft's permanent blankness
Margaret Fuller drowned within sight of land
day after day nothing solid
until I feel my fingers dissolving
I can't raise the chisel again

none of this do I confide to Father—
how watery spirits populate my sleep
rising up swollen on the sea's back
gray cobbles which I test, step
by step fearing to lose my balance
fearing their number insufficient
to take me across the indefinite
moon tempting me on
with its spliced silver rope

Finding My Master

1. *The Approach*

Every step on the stair I hope
may be Shakspere Wood returning
from John Gibson at the Caffé Greco.
My heart jumps so my shirtfront crackles
and Father looks up from his chair
where he is gilded with Roman light.
Mr. Wood has kindly offered to speak for me
bringing my anatomy degree and the two
daguerreotypes, front and profile, of *Hesper.*
She speaks better than anyone can of my worth—
mine every stroke of the chisel, every stage
from rough model to cast to
pointing and carving the pattern on stone.

Now here! Mr. Wood himself, smiling,
stammering he reports
how Gibson pushed aside his *caffé* and *panino*
to peer at *Hesper* as if to find disease.
All this time, no word escaped Gibson's lips.
My messenger in turn was studying him:
how his gaze fell on one view, then the other,
silence and a beard concealing what he thought.
Then, like something rigid snapping, he speaks.

We must come at once to his studio.
Whatever I can teach her, she shall learn.
Oh I want to embrace my Gabriel, Mr. Wood.

2. Gibson's Studio

Find first the large, worm-eaten door.
Would you think to find treasures here?
A cord with a knot for a handle
hangs from a hole. If you pull
you hear on the other side the equal
and opposite force of Mr. Gibson's bell.
Let in to a barn-like shed, you are among
gods on pedestals, horses, figures sprung
from stone. Look straight ahead
where a door like the one you entered
opens on a garden of roses, jasmine,
orange and lemon trees. You might swoon
if there weren't business to be done.

When I arrive with Father that very day
Mr. Gibson is polishing *The Wounded Amazon*'s knee.
For once I feel no urge to joke or pun.
This is a church, and Gibson close to god.
All I can say is my confession
I wish to become your pupil.
He gives his simple blessing
I will teach you all I know.

3. My Studio

Through the garden and another barn-like shed
whose central occupant is the colored *Venus*
of whom Rome talks . . . then up a flight of stairs
to the small studio which Canova himself
once occupied, I begin my Roman study
inside my master's master's room.
I the Maestro's only student
and here, first sculptor with a womb.

My First Child, and Another Daughter

Daphne, 1853; Medusa, 1854

I'll tell you why I call these children,
what they inherit from their dam.
Escaping passions of the gods
by any transformation they assert
their right to self. My Daphne becoming
laurel is herself her prize, freed from Apollo's grasp.
She didn't want to marry, nor did I.
My master praised the roundness of her flesh,
which he had never seen surpassed—
that flesh becoming its own fruit.
Her delight, like mine, in woodland sports,
the spoils of chase. What I hunt
is a place in art. I give you Daphne "arranged"
and orderly, calm in her choice.
Her father saves her, as does mine,
accepting these for grandchildren,
accepting me as wed to art.

And my second daughter in this pendant
the much-maligned Medusa whose beauty
I restore, whose hair, chief glory,
very source of charm and power, becomes
her instrument of doom. Need I say more
of how this glances off her mother?
When some men see me, they need

to make me small or queer, an elf
or pixie, a "pickle." Hair interests me,
not only Samson's source of might.
I save a lock of my sweet niece's curls
which gleam like opals to remind me
how my grizzly locks once pleased my mother.
My beautiful Medusa looks up,
lips almost part to speak, head turns
aside to see her persecutors
while her undulating hair transforms to snakes—
her strength become her jail.
In my 60s, I'll still free my hair from nets.
If observers fear it serpents, let them flee.

My First Full-Figure Daughter

Oenone, winter 1855

Of course I think of marriage
with my best friend Cornelia now wed to Lucien,
with Shakspere Wood attending
on me as we go about unchaperoned—

and my Oenone, wife abandoned
shows her grief in the burden of her form.
Her story, betrayal by Paris
choosing Helen with infamous results,
I read in Tennyson

> *with down-dropt eyes*
> *I sat alone . . .*
> *leaning on a fragment twined with vine,*
> *sang to the stillness . . .*

My Oenone's song has ended.
Just as Paris has no room for her
she overlaps her marble knoll,
right hand transmitting her sad weight
to earth, left lighting on
the shepherd's crook he left

> *A shepherd . . . but king-born.*

One bare foot rests upon the other
—now she must warm herself—
not posing, but shut inside her mood

And I was left alone within the bower; . . .
And I shall be alone until I die.

Yes, I think of marriage, and luckier
than this daughter I make my choice:
even if so inclined an artist has no
business to be married—for a man
it is well enough, but a woman
must neglect her profession or her family.

I will not die alone because a husband
alters who has called me fair a thousand times.
I tell Cornelia my Oenone occupies the same
predicament she herself would if
Lucien deserted her for me.

On Marriage,
How Many Times Must I Tell You

Each day I wake and choose my single life.
To follow art, a woman needs a wife
(I've heard you modern women say the same)
so I intimated, writing home
"I have been searching vainly for Mr. Hosmer."

Ambitious, restless spirits must be fed,
though women. Sculpture grants me motherhood
without neglect of family. I move
with no one's kind consent. Alone I carve.
I feud forever with the consolidating knot.

If I protest too much, well . . . nothing's pure
despite what Mrs. Browning swears:
that I emancipate the eccentric life
of a perfectly emancipated female, non-wife,
from all shadow of blame by the purity of mine.

You ask about my body. Five feet two,
trim waist, generous bust . . . Ah.
You mean do I love women, do I consort
with men, where do I find flesh comfort?
I thrive like a green bay tree.

Preparing for Dinner Guests, Mindful of Hatty

And the social whirl you danced in Rome
the constant visits, parties, dinners, rides—
did you have servants to pluck the hen
did they make pasta while you lifted your mallet?
I give up three days from my desk to this
dinner, not even large or complex.
Who cleared your dishes? Surely a maid to serve,
take away. Then the kitchen. Washing dishes,
restoring order while you slept or prepared
the model for your crew.
No need to keep leaping up between courses,
making sure nothing set off the smoke detector
while your guests exchanged witty remarks,
a whole unimpeded conversation
with the Brownings, with Cushman,
Hawthorne, and James. Did you ever think of class?
You didn't have to go to Europe
to meet men and women of consequence.
Can a union boss's daughter
connect with your life?
In my Rolodex, one relic remains:
"Henry Reginald Simmons, representing
Architectural Sculptors and Carvers Association"
the only business card my father ever carried,
in a little plastic sleeve,

his thick, tool-roughened fingers
fumbling to slip one out.
His masters mostly Italian—Girolami, Guarino—
except for Donnely at the Corcoran Art Gallery . . .
and Daddy the craftsman who executed designs
not the artist who conceived them, like your Master
John Gibson, and his teacher Canova. Or like you,
privileged Yankee. Where could you not go?
Part of your story is that America.
The same one that loses all accounts
of African/Chippewa Edmonia Lewis.
No whereabouts after 1883.
Caveat lector, I confess.
Preparing this dinner makes me taste
a bitter root in my story:
envy, then rage. Finally, shame.

Making Money

makes me turn from sculpting life-size women
to this mischievous, thirty-inch-tall *Puck*.
I begrudge my father who partly feigns
financial crisis to lure me back from Rome.
I will use this very noose
to untether me from Father's purse.
How could he expect I practice thrift
when what he's taught me is indulgence?
He knows nothing of the costs of marble,
managing a studio in Rome
or keeping company with giants.
Nothing will induce me
to live for the next twenty-five years in America
where I never knew that quiet or content
I have in Rome, sunrise to sunset.
Wayman Crow remains my patron
and I never lack commissions
the maddening trick, be paid as bills come due.

My little Puck, first son, some say
resembles me. He raises high a scorpion
in his palm, some say as if to throw it.
I think to demonstrate his force: scorpions
so capable of harming children, but not
this child! my devil-born god-child.
His left hand grips a lizard whose tail

ascends his arm—such as my own childish
familiars on the Charles River bank.
He wears an inverted seashell on his curls,
he's fit for flight with batwings.
So fantastical, though his sex is real.
Perching on a toadstool, one leg folded
under, the other primed to lift
his forward-leaning body braced upon that heel,
his curling toe already activates my *Puck*.
He's all potential, can spring at any moment
while the viewer turns around. Will he
hurl the scorpion? Will the curling toe be
planted as he rises to give chase?
My first *Puck* brings five hundred dollars.
I later raise the price to eight.
The Prince of Wales tours my studio
and buys a *Puck* to live with him at Oxford.
Over time, *Puck* and his brothers
earn me thirty thousand dollars.
He is called a "laugh in marble."
Supporting myself, I get the last laugh.

Rumor

*A collage of quotations: Robert and Elizabeth
Barrett Browning, Lydia Maria Child, Thomas Crawford,
John Gibson, Henry James, Frederic Leighton,
Maria Mitchell, William Story, and anonymous.*

Miss Hosmer is very willful & too independent by half.
Whatever I can teach her she shall learn.
Her voice seemed unmodulated and her manners brusque.
The queerest, best-natured little chap possible.

Whatever I shall teach her she can learn.
Hatty is compromising herself with Mr. X—What a pity!
The dearest, best-natured little chap possible.
A remarkably ugly little gray-haired boy, adorned with a
        diamond necklace.

Hatty is promising herself to Mr. X—What a pity!
She's a little rude—a good deal eccentric—but she's
        always true.
A remarkably ugly little gray-haired boy, shorn of the
        diamond necklace.
One of the frankest, bluntest, nicest little creatures that
        ever took my fancy.

She's ridden nude!—a real eccentric. What? I'm always true.
Marian knelt before Hatty & placed on her finger a ruby in
        the form of a heart.

One of the frankest, bluntest, nicest little creatures. Never
        took my fancy.
I have gained by being less ready than she to believe
        slanderous gossip.

Marian knelt before Hatty & placed on her finger a ruby,
        from her heart.
Miss Hosmer's want of modesty is enough to disgust a dog.
I remained less ready than she to grieve at slanderous gossip.
She worked in secret. She had few confidants.

Miss Hosmer wants modesty enough. Disgusting frog.
Her voice seemed unmodulated and her manners risqué.
She worked in secret. She had new confidence.
Miss Hosmer is very skillful but too independent by half.

Astronomer Maria Mitchell
Meets Harriet Hosmer

Rome, sculptor Paul Akers' studio

In strides the pretty girl,
her hands thrust in her pockets,
and begins to rattle
an invitation to ride horseback
over the Campagna, which he interrupts
Oh, not with you—I'm afraid to.

So this is Harriet Hosmer.
She is not like us Quakers.
At first troubled by her ways
I later see that she parades
her weaknesses with the conscious power
of one who knows her strength.

She possesses psychic gifts.
When objects vanish, she tells the owner
where they hide. One day out riding
she saw a fence post raise itself
above the ground. In these matters
I try to keep my mind ajar.

Pity her three male friends in Iowa
who boasted men are better climbers.
That summer day she beat them to the top
of what they named Mt. Hosmer.

I do not wonder that she plans
to carve the ancient Queen Zenobia,
once mistress of the Roman East.
Even vanquished, on display in Rome
Zenobia would not bow her regal shoulders,
in captive dignity strode on.

How Miss Hosmer studies to make the woman
express her people's fate.
She learns the gaze from ancient coins.
If she hears that in a church

two hundred miles away she will find
the robes of Eastern Queens
she mounts her horse and rides to see.

In all America no school
would teach Miss Hosmer sculpture.
I think she rules in exile too.

To Hatty on Easter Sunday, Among Spirits

I read how on your moonlight ride alone
from Lexington, your first meeting
with Lydia Maria Child,
the fence rail rose vertical
before you. Awed, not fearful,
you "most religiously" viewed it.

Then the "curious incident" in Rome:
having just lain down you felt impelled
to say aloud to Cornelia "I have such a
feeling of a carriage accident."
She said you'd been dreaming; nothing
of the sort, you answered, repeating
your premonition. Ten minutes later
a "tremendous crash" under your windows:
the princess Orsini's carriage upside down,
her face cut by broken glass, she pulled
through the window in her red evening gown
and you concluding "see what a witch I am."

Among your friends you gained a reputation
for the inner flashes that showed you
where lost articles hid—Lady Ashburton's key,
her despatch box already sought and overlooked
in the bank where you saw it
buried in your head.

Your maid Rosa ill with the familiar consumption—
just after visiting her you slept,
waking at five to hear the clock strike
and Rosa appearing from behind the screen
in your bedroom. *"Adesso sono contento,
adesso sono felice"* she told you,
then was gone. You sprang up
searched behind the screen, the curtains
. . . then recalled your door was locked
and recognized a vision.
The messenger you sent returned with news
Rosa had died at five o'clock.
That experience you said was real
as any of your life.

When my blue brother Gary was born
with a hole in his heart
my mother woke in the middle of the night
to find her own mother, years departed,
at the foot of her hospital bed
announcing "I'm going to take him with me"
and five days later kept her word.

I once opened the front door
into an empty house and heard
the piano play a chord
the very hour a transatlantic plane I was to meet
had lost an engine and turned back.
Just this winter at my desk

a sudden dagger in my lower back bent me over
for no reason, just at noon when my friend
three thousand miles away sprawled on the ice
with a fractured hip.
I view these almost religiously . . .

Hatty, meet me in the lily's chalice,
on golden powder, rise

Beginning and Ending with Mahler's *Kindertotenlieder*

for Gary Edward Simmons,
September 14–21, 1947

Look at us well, for soon we will be far away.

Eyes closed, hypothetical blue.
Red hair, silk threads woven into a cap
across the fontanelle
that wouldn't need to grow hard.
Tiny fingers arranged at your sides
on the white cover, nails perfect abalone.

A "blue baby" they said
but your skin looked pink to me.
Was it makeup? the same disguise
I've seen on aunts and uncles,
on our father. *Our.*

I never saw you breathe
but I watched you traverse
the globe of our mother's belly,
placed my hand on your tour.
I didn't look well enough
to last this half-century.

Two years later, they could do the Blalock procedure
and fix the traitor valve.
Our sister never saw you even once.
I befriend men named Gary.
Live infants sleep with their hands up
as if, about to be robbed, they surrender.

You've taken a walk to the hills over there, merely gone ahead.

Her Story, My Daughter Beatrice

Beatrice Cenci, 1856

The Secret Archives of the Vatican contain
a manuscript from 1599—the trial
for parricide of Giacomo and Beatrice Cenci
the ill-used children, and their stepmother Lucrezia.
The Pope shows poorly in this daughter's tale
of incest. She wrote him more than once
complaining of her father. No response.
The same Count Cenci her father, convicted
sodomist, bought pardons and enriched the Church.

How many ways for a daughter to be abused—
by lustful gods, by errant husbands—even
by her father. The Count with threats and force
took Beatrice to his bed, telling her
this new heresy: that when a father
used his daughter thus, the saints were born.
Sometimes he moved the family to a grim
outpost-castle, La Rocca Petrella,
where he locked them, used them as he willed.
No earthly rescue but what they'd themselves devise:
the murder of him who kept them in his hell.

We do but that which 'twere a deadly crime
to leave undone.

But the murderers were found, the plotters condemned.
Even Farinaccio's defense

based on the Count's incestuous abuse
failed to save Beatrice's life. Beheaded,
she and Lucrezia; Giacomo clubbed to death:
such the clemency of Clement VIII.
The Church put in its thumb and pulled out
the dead Count's riches, that plum,
and said What a good boy am I.

My marble daughter's figure speaks her piece.

Now he is dead I can sleep face down
my back turned on all possible harm.
I have not slept so easy since before I bled.
I sleep soundly though tomorrow I wake
to my last dawn, last clover-sweetened air.
I fold one leg to my chest as in the womb,
the other stretches out, toes at the edge
of my world. One slipper shows, trimmed
with ribbons and lace. These slippers I will leave
before I climb the stairs to my beheading.
My gown slips like water off one shoulder,
its folds cascade down my terraced pallet.
A mother gave my head a pillow
and I give myself human comfort, my right
hand beneath my cheek. The other
holds a rosary. My faith is strong although
the crimes which my tongue dared to name
God did not scruple to avenge, except through me.

I therefore sleep. You, watching—grant
the mercy that my judges have denied.

Beatrice Dreams

The sisters visited my studio, and one said of
Beatrice, "How well she sleeps." "No," said
the other, "How well she dreams."

The sea beneath me folds its robes
while mine stream out to grab
the draft, to soar above the mob

that comes to watch me climb the stair
consign me ever into air
a circling route of zone and sphere

where none can hide, lock, cage
a child to split her, pour in rage
with clenched teeth and rolling gaze

and none may point to me to find
how many knots he drifts from land—
I stitch my compass on the wind

Hatty's Anxiety Dream

This time my bones are broken and re-set
stretched to form a taller me
one they will never call little
taller than Powers or Canova
tall as my master

and when the wires stretched between
the gaps to enlarge me
communicate x's
when the wires are twisted and laced
my form will not shake

then a hand
from the corner lifts its baton
and the wires grow wings
butterflies that pulse and lift
filling the room with stained glass

a pile of kindling
beside a watered silk gown

Tomb of Judith Falconnet:
Sant' Andrea Delle Fratte, Rome

This commission makes me the first
American artist with sculpture in a Roman church.
I endeavor to exhaust myself on the work,
using the sixteen-year-old's death mask
and a portrait bust of her in life
to capture for her mother the child's
true face. On a couch I lay her down
asleep as for an hour, her hands relaxed—
in one a rosary, the other tranquil at her side.
She turns her head out toward the chapel to show
that no bad dreams assault her peace.
Untroubled, calm, with light across her face . . .

like sister Helen, her bed in the bay window
head turned to father and me to tell us
with her eyes what none of us would speak
then she's beyond crying out, beyond the roiling chest
her fever setting through pinholes in the dark, she's calm
—I want to shake you from unfeeling, selfish stillness!—

I lay my hand inside the cool, white palm.

Today, Sant'Andrea Delle Fratte

At evening mass, we wander in to find
your *Judith Falconnet*. One Bernini angel
swirls toward us from the altar; the other
covers himself to be restored. The priest intones.
Mothers with crinkly shopping bags bless
themselves and kneel, dragging toddlers.
Men just finished work drift in.
I'm standing near a chapel when a couple
turns to me expecting something and I
throw up my hands, empty as my comprehension.
It's dark in here: scaffolding
hides windows on the west facade,
more restoration. The Father spreads his arms
to bless us standing where you, Hatty, stood
pleased with your creation, pleased with what
you called magnificent light on Judith sleeping
underneath an arch, opposite another artist's
crude evocation of the Angel of Death.
Mass ends, and from the cloister a wave
of orange blossoms transports us . . .
1857 . . .
    or medieval Rome where this church
marked town's limit, sacred and profane.
All around it nettles grew, greens for believers
when the shoots were young.

Purification

Today walking to my studio, down
the Spanish Steps beside Keats' house
I see the sun go gray as flames surround
a pile of chairs and tables heaped like corpses
naked on the cobblestones below that room
where the unbearable, uncommon brightness
of his eyes went out and Gherardi, silent, came
to cast the death mask that would lie encased
for visitors to see a hundred years from then
beside the manuscript in Keats' hand
where sleep, sweet dreams, and quiet breathing
name both the poet's illness and its end . . .
like mother's . . . *some shape of beauty moves away*
the pall and moves me through the flames.

To Hatty, on Boils

Trying surgery on my own
axilla where a pearl has grown inside a red ring
I think of the plague of your boils.
"Axilla" because the armpit is the butt
of bad jokes: those places in the body no
one wants to visit, Latin ornaments.

I hereby dignify the armpit redolent of labor,
little cave where we dare admit lovers;
and the butt on which you couldn't sit.
You railed against prostration
like Pallas Athena of the Vatican on a sofa.
United in pus, I salute you.

Byl byle bile bule boyl
and farther back to *carbunculus*
the deep-red garnet, the glowing coal;
furunculus the petty thief, vine knob
that steals the sap from branches . . .
still earlier, plundering our brother Job.

We are part of a long line of bacteria inns
soft and pigmented, infinitely digestible.
Hospitable planets, we revolve around ourselves,
we rotate like sucklings on a spit. Patience.
Let the microbes feast, within good taste's limits.
We are all soon cured.

My Clothes

". . . for my part, I give her full leave to wear
what may suit her best, and to behave
as her inner woman prompts."

—Nathaniel Hawthorne,
Notebooks, April 13, 1858

He gives me full leave. Ha! Need I ask his yea?
Why so preoccupied with my appearance?
I can't recall writing home of his.
Yes, Virginia: I am aware that we are, perhaps,
the most discussed animal in the universe . . .
He sees fit to comment on my cravat and shirtfront,
my short-cropped curls; he can't imagine
I might terminate in a petticoat
any more than in a fish's tail.
And if I don't? I dress to climb a scaffold,
meet Thomas Hart Benton at eye-level
in knee-high skirt with knickers underneath.
I dress in sympathetic Zouave trousers
for my Zenobia, Palmyra's exiled queen.
Let none report I don't love finery:
silks, plumage, rubies, and Etruscan gold.
Listen—I wear exactly what I choose.
Meeting visitors to my Roman studio
I slip my hands inside my pockets
as convention says that boys are wont to do.
To some, I seem a charming hybrid

of energetic young lady and modest lad.
Saluting friends from a carriage, I touch my hat
and raise it, gentlemanly fashion.
Nathaniel, you claim to understand how Rome
gives American artists necessary freedom—
you almost bear the queerness of my clothes,
excusable in a young woman, questionable beyond.
Meanwhile you fixate on my petticoats,
maintaining that you do not *look so low.*
Someday they'll write about the problematic
phallic woman. I wear
whatever my will for action may demand.
Such as, that night in Florence with Robert Browning
I donned his clothes to gain the unhooped precincts
of Certosa Convent, see exquisite Donatellos.
I even stood with monks inside their cells!—
the cloister's walls held firm, the monks still prayed.
You write that I am brisk, wide-awake.
What did you expect? Ah well . . .
Among animals, *one* has a sense of humor.

Hatty Revises Current Fashion

Ladies! No more English bang or fringe.
If you want classic oval contours
erase that severing straight line.
Remove your corsets. Enjoy
the *Venus de Milo*'s splendid girth.
High art requires big ankles too—
how can a beautiful strong form
lurch on a wispy pedestal?
Above all, no more little claws.
Square fingers with straight-line nails.
Imagine my wielding the chisel
with nails that enfeeble my grip
or catch on rough stone.
Let your hands tell a story
of strength first—on this
later beauty may be based.
My final argument? Regard
the even nails of those two wedded poets
in my cast of their clasped hands.

Zenobia Speaks, in Chains and Free

Day and night I form inside my maker
as my shape inhabits stone.
She lives with tales of me these months
researching coins and dress,
my origins—Arab? Jewish? Kin to
Cleopatra? She reads aloofness from my king
except for procreation, my reign
for six years following his death
till my defeat by Emperor Aurelian.
She rejects historical accounts
of me so weighted down by chains
attendants must lift them for me.
I stand tall at seven feet—
she moves from Gibson's studio to her own
to carve her largest figure yet:
me vertical, not curled inside
a private world, but carrying my chain
in one strong hand.
Not naked before the conqueror
but shielded, stationed in my garments.
My parted feet absorb the movement
of the earth which jolts me
from Palmyra to the enemy's Rome.
My gaze is downcast but my shoulders
square; I've filled my lungs to raise them,

match the crown that I still own.
I'm gazing down because why try
to see a friend in all that company
watching what the conqueror brings home?
The chain I bear might stave an emperor off.
This Zenobia is no one's slave,
will not stretch supine on a Roman couch.
Are you ready, world, for such a Queen?
Such a woman, who holds her freedom
in her own mind?

The Critics Comment on *Zenobia*

If it were the work of a man, it would be considered more than clever; but as it is from the chisel of a woman, why, it is an *innovation*.

Hosmer and any other women who feel the desire for work stirring within them should be true to their characteristic gift and use their time decorating buildings with sculptured flower-and-leaf ornament instead of making ideal sculptures.

That head is bowed only because she is a woman, and she will not give the look of love to the man who has forced her after him . . . She is a *lady*, and knows that there is something higher than joy or pain.

The statue tells its story most successfully. It lives and moves with the solemn grace of a dethroned Queen. I know enough of the sculptor's art to recognize the labor, as well as talent, which Miss Hosmer must have brought to this masterpiece, not only in its original conception, but in the details of its execution. I rejoice in such a work by an American artist . . .

In dealing with this subject Miss Hosmer has united womanly dignity and delicacy, with the best qualities of the masculine hand.

Zenobia is not Hosmer's work at all but that of an Italian workman at Rome.

The Queen of the East gives audience, for she has arisen again under the loving hands of a woman. The Queen is Zenobia, and the woman is Harriet Hosmer. It is of the one rather than the other, we write to-day. And we want to tell you of a delicate little New England girl . . .

Zenobia . . . Yonder there is left for thee
A palace-garden in the purple wall
Of those calm hills to close thy destiny . . .
Thou shall learn to love and hate the throne
That robs an empire but repays a home.

I Fight the Battle of the Amazons

How dare they take their mallets to my reputation?
Two articles in *Art Journal* and the *Queen*
print their accusation *The Zenobia*
is said to be by Miss Hosmer—but really
executed by an Italian workman in Rome.
No mere coincidence that my detractors get
so bold following the show at Crystal Palace
of my strongest daughter yet, the exiled queen.
If to modulate my voice means bear
injustice silently, I reject that female wile.
What has been whispered seven years
can now be read, hence cause for libel suit.
Meanwhile my response in print explains
We women artists have no objection
to its being known that we employ
assistants; we merely object to its being supposed
that it is a system peculiar to ourselves.
My own hands studied long and finished the *Zenobia*.
Gibson and Story take my side
in print so that the editor of the *Queen* must
take seriously my suit for damages of a thousand pounds.
I call her "he"—he offers to print any apology
I dictate if I'll drop my suit. I demand
he publish such admissions

in *The Times* and *Galignani* as well as in the *Queen*.
A woman artist honored by frequent commissions
is an object of peculiar odium—sometimes to her sex.
They won't send me so simply into exile.
I give you graphic proof: this picture taken
in my studio, entitled "Hosmer and Her Men."
At the center of two dozen workmen,
I stand, arms folded—a sultan with her harem.

Thomas Hart Benton, in Bronze

Lafayette Park, St. Louis, Missouri

May I not be allowed to gloat?
Not for nothing did I carry Benton's picture
in my watch two years awaiting word.
Getting the commission
from the three-man panel—yes, that's *man*
not person—appointed by the state legislature.
This after Headley, friend
to sculptor Stone (I call him Pebbly), wrote me
hoping I'd withdraw my name. What
were my intentions, he inquired.
I answered him: to get the prize.

True, my patron Crow was one of the decisive three.
The sketch I sent him from Rome
presumed drowned with all aboard the ship
whose mailbag, *grazie*, was recovered.
I choose to dress the statesman in the cloak
he truly wore—no Roman toga—
but not in hat and vest
as if he's just come from the haberdasher.
Bareheaded to the elements, a great man
ten feet tall, head bowed in thought
and recognizing all who'll seek to meet
those steady eyes. His hands

unfurl a map suggested by his words
There is the East. There is India.

My letter of acceptance to the committee
anticipates the familiar cry from critics
and competitors. I praise my teacher
of anatomy, my patron's home
now this source of public recognition.
I have reason to be grateful to you, because
I am a woman and knowing
what barriers must in the outset
oppose all womanly efforts, I am indebted
to the chivalry of the West, which has first
overleaped them . . . Your kindness will now
afford me opportunity of proving to what
rank I am entitled as an artist . . .
for this work must be, as we understand
the term, a manly *work, and hence*
its merit alone must be my defense
against the attacks of those who
stand ready to resist any encroachment
upon their self-appropriated sphere.

I commence the model, an overwhelming
mass of clay. Completed, the subject
will rise ten feet upon a granite pedestal
which adds another four. As I work
atop a stair that reaches to his knee

my head almost achieves his shoulder.
My own costume, Zouave trousers, keeps me
from tripping on useless skirts.
Like any artist, I cannot say how soon
the statue will be finished. When
I have made the model it must be transported
to Munich's Royal Foundry, cast in bronze,
then shipped across the ocean to its home—
ten thousand dollars in gold the total fee.

Eight years until the *Benton* is unveiled,
May 27, 1868 proclaimed a city holiday.
Forty thousand in attendance as his daughter
pulls the cord and shows the bronze
that's caught for time, she says, her father's look.
I know how slippery the public and critic's
fancy but the worst I hear about is muttered,
my Benton looks instead like Wayman Crow.
No one praises or blames
the statue for its woman maker who carved
a man for public monument—the world inverted.
Dwarfed I stood beside him. Yet he fit
inside my mind, inside my hands.

Astoria, New York Interlude:
Italian Notebook

I.

Bruno, husband of Maria, son-in-law
of Giuseppe Marino, sitting on our couch
extols Puccini whom my parents never heard of
and I just heard in Music 101.
In his half-good tenor voice, Bruno
gives us excerpts of his favorite arias
from *La Bohème, Madame Butterfly*, tears
brimming as he sings. Mr. Marino
a stonecarver like my father, but schooled
in the old country to execute angels and saints
by pointing—or "pernting" as my father says.
How mathematical my dropout father had to be.

II.

Tough Patty Saporito from Thirty-Third Street:
her mother prematurely white, or maybe
older than Luigi her rakish, mustached husband
who one night when I am sleeping over
comes home late full of red wine
and throws up in the sink. Next day
we visit their relatives with a yard blessed
by Mary and assorted saints to watch the vegetables
and baby cousins staggering along the rows,

beyond fatigue by nightfall when the uncles
start to sing. So different from mine,
the dour, unmarried uncles and aunts cohabiting
in silence. They need music, pasta, wine
—not boiled meat and dry potatoes.

III.

Rose Cicogna, my friend Rosie's mother
cooks strange food we almost never eat.
We eat corned beef or other fatty flesh.
I feed mine to the dog under the table.
Dumb, she shows all over what she's won.
Or I wrap the half-chewed clumps
inside my napkin, flush them later.
Rosie's mother, the only braless mother
I know, sometimes lifts a breast
onto her forearm for mechanical support.
Rosie's mother always worries, later
has a breakdown. Her sister Anna visits
and they tell secrets in Italian.
One afternoon Rosie's mother comes home
finds Rosie, proud of her budding,
prancing naked before two girlfriends
who didn't take the dare.
How far from Italy, our Thirty-Second Street
cement and asphalt. No tomatoes, eggplant,
basil, grapes. Rosie's mother's food's
my favorite now—farther back than yuppies,

marathoners, back down the cracked
pavement to Rosie's mother.
Rose at the sink rinsing dinner pasta,
a white apron over her flowered dress,
her dark curls twisting onto her brow,
our faces in the window going up in steam.

I Tell Hatty the Effacing Dream

When the rogue wave rolled through
the open window over my desk
and onto my handwritten pages
the words blurred, merged
with the sea, and swam away.

I tried writing a protest
but the sea wrote
silence, go under, join the horizon
over my words.

Your works, cataloged
by a Watertown priest
earning his library degree,
how often he lists them
Location Unknown.

I here write your lost children home—
    the head of *Byron, The Falling Star,*
    Caesar the dog, *The Bridge of Sighs,*
    Phosper and Hesper, Triton Fountain,
    Fountain of the Siren, The Staghound,
    Hylas and the Water Nymphs,
    Queen Isabella of Castile, Maria Sophia Queen of Naples,
    Morning and the Setting of the Stars,
    The Waking Faun …

Now. Let the sea come.

Stonecarver, Restoring

Henry Reginald Simmons,
Soldiers and Sailors Monument, 1960

He kneels on top of Manhattan
turning his chisel in the eye
so the eagle can see again.

One hundred fifteen feet up, man
and bird are a single gray
animal, perched on Manhattan

where nothing reaches but rain
and the city's breath. Vandals can't fly.
When the eagle sees again

it will watch George Washington
thrown piecemeal from a horse. Today
while he's kneeling here, a Manhattan

kid with a dealer downtown
is selling Columbus's arm for a high.
But this eagle will see again.

The stonecarver remembers his Latin—
Nil desperandum—and why
he kneels on top of Manhattan
so the eagle can see again.

Flesh and Stone

Today I consider your treatment
of the female body in stone
the stories that you tell
and another kind of body-carving

young women with X-Acto knives
tracing paths across their abdomens
I saw firsthand these scars
on a woman in Emergency
examined by the resident
and my student tells me
"cutters" testify before her psych class
they feel relief in opening
those envelopes of flesh . . .

the world must end
that fears and captivates
those women's bodies
that looks in wonderment
then looks away

let women with sharp instruments
follow you
and find relief in opening stone

Thinking, Making Ready

I am thinking of you Hatty
as I make ready to let
the camera see into my breast
search for marauders
stupid parasites destroying their host
I am thinking of the surgeon's knife
describing a semi-circle, peeling back
a flap to follow road signs, wires
planted to mark the limits
of health, I am thinking
of you lifting your chisel
shaping the left breast of Oenone
polishing the nipple that barely
shows behind her arm, I am
thinking of your aunt who died of
cancer your "one horror"
and your lack of faith in cures
I am thinking of Charlotte Cushman
told that her "trouble"
breast cancer had been aggravated
by the act of writing
as her flesh rubbed against
the bones of her corsets
(if only she had just sat still!)
I am thinking of women's breasts

yours and mine, my sister's
daughter's, friends' rubbing
against corporate profit, elemental poisons
thinking of Cushman's treatment
abscesses, pneumonia—
forty-one days after surgery
her incision not closed

Hatty to Posterity:
On Friendship, Flirtation, and the Fury to Wed

You will have to unravel this vine, which to avoid
being lonely braids itself into inscrutable knots.
My most likely mate, they say, was Shakspere Wood

three years older, in Rome from the Royal Academy.
A friend feared I was compromising
myself with him. Friendship only, I say;

generous aid to Miss Cushman and me. Yes, we rode
out together. You saw us dancing
often at the great subscription ball, poor Mr. Wood

whose mismatched feet made comic our waltz.
But I cherish laughter—and no stumbling in his
business sense or in his lectures on the arts.

Browning? He craved female company, but stayed true
to his Ba. Yes, we shared adventures—the runaway cart
in Florence, the illicit convent tour. So?

They both called me darling and pet. Women
companions conversing with Robert often found
themselves pressed to the extreme of the divan.

Well, what *of* Fay Leighton? Most
elegant man to enter my studio, my life
—but always in love with Adelaide.

When he first paused at the top of my stair
asking *"E permeso?"* my heart somersaulted:
a Raphael painting breathed air.

He wrote me *Beloved my Hat* signing off
with a sketch labelled *This is the kiss . . .*
Yours always, Fay. Preference made him safe.

My jest: when not at work, I flirted
with any beauty to delight me, he or she
I loved a lover howling at the gate.

But Louisa, my Juno, singular
since first she dazzled me at Melchet Court
my goddess of the ebony hair,

mid thunderclouds those lightning eyes . . .
I called her *sposa,*
myself her hubbie or wedded wife.

More cunning knots we wove one winter
in my apartment in Rome—she the Ma,
I fat sister to her thirteen-year-old daughter.

Posterity, solve on   how I sent clover to the world.

Permanent Magnets

for Louisa, Lady Ashburton, 1875

I did not name the force
    that kept me spinning
        one direction like electrons
in a lodestone's atoms.
    All my arrows pointed
        to you beloved Lady
and your daughter—together more
    than my lost mother and sister.
        Few substances can sustain
a magnetic field, electric charge
    in motion: your eyes on me
        my hands on you,
what you called "treatment"
    I will accept any treatment at your hands!
    I know what kind it would be.
Such as I called Laocoöning—
    one old story says the priest was punished
        for sleeping with his wife
before Apollo's image. They said . . . I say . . .
    What matter. I strove
        for a machine to solve
with magnets the problem
    of perpetual stillness.
        To keep you whispering in my ear.

My Rome, Vanishing

1870 onward

Vittorio Emanuele's Republican Army
shooting musket balls past my ear,
the man beside me hit, losing fingers—
I take him into my house, bandage him
as best I can—real blood
and flesh, not broken marble.

My Rome changed forever, now tinsel
and vulgarity, her calm majesty gone.
Art changes too, as students look to Paris
for study. Soon the grotesque
caricaturing nature will be "original,"
butcher and baker will replace
Michelangelo for inspiration.

Once I was nearly killed on the Caccia
riding Bruno, thrown and dragged,
my foot in the stirrup. I calmly urged
but he did not stop; neither did he run—
thus sparing me while I dislodged my foot
and rolled off, safe. Now I am thrown

by alteration. I climbed back onto Bruno
but cannot remount my Rome
and finish the chase.

Though I will call it home for years still
I will become a bird of passage
flying from Via Margutta,
from the dear Italian tongue
that sounds to me as natural as English,
the pure art, the Campagna, the grave of my master.

I stand on Via delle Quattro Fontane
close by my rooms, fancying I see
what lies ahead in this spot

a Yu Yuan Ristorante, Cinese
a dark facade named "The Edge"
and in one of the four sculptured fountains
commissioned by Pope Sixtus to mark the holy crossroads
a goddess reclines, head propped on her right hand
arm bent at the elbow . . .
between her breast and crooked arm
someone has propped an empty Dom Perignon

When one has lived in Rome
there is no other place afterwards.
I will always return
but visitors are strangers.
And my Rome sets
like the evening star over
the Campidoglio.

Crossing Zones

The School for Studij di Pintura e Scultura
still instructs apprentices in art
across Margutta from your studio.
A grapevine trained to arch across the street
defines this narrow space for art, against
the Lancias and Vespas making time.
Here now antiques, furniture refinishing,
Oriental rugs, a sculpture studio. A fabric shop
at number 5 where you once wielded hammer
mingling with the sounds of work that rose
above these cobblestones, and carriage traffic
to cedars on the Pincio, the one
of Rome's seven hills that you could see.
Today, someone's still hammering,
material resists the bite of an electric saw.
Are you upstairs at 116? Is that your
horse-drawn carriage waiting at the corner
beside the salmon-colored wall?
What do you think, rounding that corner
to come upon Margutta Vegetariano at 119,
the motto *cave carnem?*
You might long for meat, being
by your own account a voracious eater.
But you're here over greens with us,

watching the man leave his wife
four times to talk on a cell phone.
Nearby, two Roman women with briefcases
slip their shoes off underneath the table.
Take yours off, too—your feet must hurt—
and try this *melanzane,* this *frutta di bosco.*

Parallel Universes

for Sue, in Florence
and thinking of Hatty at the Charles River, her rats

I had to laugh when the kids
on the Ponte Vecchio overlooking the Arno
pointed and yelled, pronounced
in three languages RAT
and you turned to me, insisting
it must be an otter.
Me a New York kid who'd perched
on the wall in Astoria Park
looking down at rocks edging
the East River, I saw what
swam at the edges of playgrounds,
what scrambled up to eat.
Otter! I didn't even hear the word
till I was thirty, much less see one
except for *Nature* on TV.
Did you really mean there were otters
in that Ohio town where you grew up
in a private house fully insured?
As foreign to me as rats to you:
that moment when your father handed
your high school boyfriend the key

to his new convertible and said *Drive.*
That June day I was riding the BMT
at rush hour when some guy
lifted the wallet from my bag,
stroked through the crowd, out
and down the platform
as the doors shut again and the train
slid under the river.

I Rededicate Watertown's
Hosmer School to You, Hatty

since you're the one whose children we visit at the Met,
the MFA, the Wadsworth Athenaeum, that church
            in Rome—
to name a few.
            Do you demur? Your father and cousin, those
good doctors of Watertown, deserved the honor?
Sorry, I refuse to be deterred.

Let students in their labs concoct your patented
            artificial marble.
In art classes, give them calipers and pointers, clay
            and plaster;
let them form models, cast them. Let them cut the stones
they fabricate in chemistry. Bring them on field trips,
            let them
touch the squirmy slippery creatures, no cries of *ew!*
Let none retreat from the dissecting table.
Give them magnets to work motors, let them learn all
moving parts, how to draw and use them.
Let them read old stories, conjure new ones for their age.
And let them laugh. If someone tells them
No you may not study that
let them rejoice to get expelled three times, like you.

Hatty's Dream, 1902

I ride my favorite hunter Bruno
by moonlight to the ancient battleground
where we must twist and turn

around my loves all gathered there
who lift their faces as we pass
Oh moon, mother us with patience

and at the heart of vines and poppies
anointed with light the new King Edward
ascended on his throne

beside him my Louisa in her wheelchair
the paisley shawl around her
my beloved Amazon

I dismount, surround her with my arms
draw from my pocket the clay
and begin to shape her a breast

I Didn't Want to Admit It

How you abandoned sculpture for machinery,
the seventies and eighties blanks or lost,
your last known major work in 1894.
And the comedown of coming home.
One theory says the neoclassical went out of style
one says you over-partied

one says you didn't heed your own advice,
married Lady A. and gave up art.
One says you always were mechanical,
no surprise you labored thirty years
on a perpetual motion machine using magnets,
patented your artificial marble.

    Shall I add mine to the theories as you added
        ingredients
    to that marble's petrifying, dyeing bath?

You said anyone could sculpt—
unique, a perpetual motion machine.
Its magnets spun wheels like fortunes but couldn't
repel Mother and Helen's TB, Louisa's breast cancer,
Maysie's fatal disease. Impossible
machine kept only you moving on.

Here add indigo to the mix.
Blue is composed of Indigo, nitric acid, and alum-—
the indigo
is proportional to the brilliance of color desired
& any color which the dyes can invent may be given.

You returned to Watertown almost unnoticed:
"I have not seen her since her return to America";
you gave up "almost everything, even the society
of her dearest friends for her work on perpetual motion."
Boarded with the jeweler and his family—
no parties, riding out, royal friends.

Everyone had called you sprite, elf.
You joked and made them laugh,
locked your feelings behind news.
"Hatty is such a bad correspondent in personal matters . . ."
Even you wrote of the faun with your face
"Fauns don't get angry you know."

> *I have my claim to a patent upon this*
> *improvement—viz.*
> *That the central portion of the stone, whatever*
> *its diameter,*
> *is of equal hardness with the outer surface.*

No late photos of you at work with magnets,
no notes or drawings for your machine. Only bills

in Probate records. It took two years to try
and fail to pay your debts—Materials & Labor on Machine,
Labor on Machine, Labor on Machine. Money advanced
to pay nurses, Board, etc. in last sickness, Medicines,
              Medical services.

I've confessed, now you: Did you really want most
to set an engine going forever?
Not to pick up your first tools, wet the dried clay, and begin?

The stone now passes into the hands of the polisher . . .

Brief Letter from Hatty,
and Author's Response

Dear Ms. Oles,

Having just read your so-called
admission, I am impelled to set you right.
Everyone who knew me told a single tale:
my merriment and brightness; exuberance of spirits,
care-free as a child. Now who are you,
by what clairvoyance do you find such shadows?
Do you not gaze within yourself?

Yours,
Harriet G. Hosmer

August 15, 2005

Dear Hatty,

Just so!—to find what all denied.
Consoling thought, but science teaches
children aren't care-free.
I grant you chords of every music,
carve of you our greatest model
Hatty Victrix
for viewing in the round.

Yours,
Carole

The Tenth Muse

The Tenth Muse is Work
and the Other Nine are helpless without her.
So I stood twelve hours a day
wielding chisel, waking stone.
Was it that adamantine, my will
to prove a woman's

power to carve as well as men?
Not exactly. I wanted to work
at what I loved—to capture and still
the moving parts of creatures, hold Mother
Nature's bounty in stone.
I learned more in a Roman day

than in years at home. I'd left my former body
and found another now truly mine.
Perhaps why I evoked in stone
those moments, the nether
land of day and night, waking and sleeping—works
like my step poising on the sill.

Often I carved pairs or pendants, my will
for a mate showing through long days
for art. I envied the married their years together

despite my companions, women and men.
I joked that if I didn't work,
I flirted. Either would keep me from being alone,

dwelling on sorrows I couldn't speak to anyone.
Stone could transmute them, stone and my will.
Then I lost the Lincoln competition, couldn't work
as before the judges' nay.
Help came from the dearest woman,
patron more than thirty years, her

with whom I stayed in England, Rome—mother
and friend. Small sculptures in stone
those decades. But inventions, lectures, women's
rights. I stayed when she was mortally ill.
The Waking Faun my double is clay—
a fragile, lost work.

No mother, the Tenth Muse will make no promises.
Stone I carved to last illumined my days,
and this woman's work perturbed the dense air.

February 21, Then and Now

with excerpts from HH's letters

This is the day the long shadow
swallowed, day you dreamed for yourself
a monument of yellow marble,
two black horses pulling the carriage.
I think of your deathday early
as I drive to have the basal cell
burned off my left temple again.
I think of it listening to NPR,
Garrison Keillor's litany of who
else claims this day

    O fateful Hours! the least
    Of whom comes pregnant with a life or death

the births of Pauline Kael,
Anaïs Nin, Andrés Segovia; *The New Yorker.*
The death by assassination
of Malcolm X in 1965,
fifty-seven years after you perceived

    that upward tendency in my toes

Now I perceive myself part of time:
yours, mine, my children's . . . the whole
march across creation's brow . . . unless
we ourselves wreck the earth.

Were you ready at seventy-eight,
having worked the last two decades
on your perpetual motion machine,
ready to catch cold forever, stop?

*It is quite frightful to see how time runs on
and how short are the days to work in*

You meant the days for sculpting,
twelve hours of continuous standing to work
not enough, and still you reminded yourself

pazienza, col tempo tutto forse

You meant the days for sculpting
but later left art, preferring
the search for that endless machine.
Or maybe you tired.
Yet your art gives perpetual motion,
resurrects you to canter in Boston, on the Campagna,
to my dermatologist off the Esplanade.

I will follow your cleaning instructions

*perhaps a very gentle scrubbing—the ammonia
in fresh rainwater . . . After that the marble should
be rubbed over with fine marble dust*

Hatty, not contained by Lot 3747
on Hemlock at Lily, Mt. Auburn Cemetery,
with your bone dust
let me polish your children.

Harriet Hosmer with her sculpture *Thomas Hart Benton,*
photographed by Mariannecci, Rome.
Photograph courtesy of The Schlesinger Library,
Radcliffe Institute, Harvard University.

AFTERWORD:
ON SERENDIPITY

When I recently read some poems from *Waking Stone* at a local art gallery, the announcement of the event elicited an e-mail message from my colleague Laird Easton in the History Department at California State University, Chico. It emerged that the Elizabeth Clementine Kinney who was among the plotters of Hosmer's first attempt to breach the walls of Certosa Convent was his great-great-grandmother. A published author of articles and poems, Kinney recounts the event in her memoir in manuscript; her papers are collected at Columbia University Library in New York City. (See Sherwood 113–14 and notes 34 and 35 to "Chapter 9: Womanly Concerns and Girlish Escapades," 347.)

NOTES

My two basic sources for information about Harriet Hosmer are *Harriet Hosmer: Letters and Memories,* ed. Cornelia Carr (New York: Moffat, Yard & Co., 1912) and Dolly Sherwood's *Harriet Hosmer American Sculptor 1830–1908* (Columbia and London: University of Missouri Press, 1991). The following notes cite additional sources and identify direct quotations and references. Many of these materials are in The Schlesinger Library at Radcliffe Institute for Advanced Study, Harvard University, hereafter identified as SL.

"I Am Lowered, I Am Raised" contains an anachronistic reference to Emily Dickinson, whose poetry I imagine Hosmer to know in this context.

"That Other River, the Mississippi" refers to Cornelia Crow, daughter of Hosmer's eventual patron, Wayman Crow and a classmate at Mrs. Sedgwick's School. Hosmer did own a gun and knew how to shoot it.

"More Wildlife Study" is based on the undocumented *Notes of Travel and Life: By Two Ladies—Misses Mendell and Hosmer,* "Published in NY for the authors, 1854" found in the Watertown, Massachusetts Public Library's Hosmer archives. Father Joseph Curran, Hosmer scholar, believes it authentic but is unable to identify Miss Mendell and other references.

"Linkage" records Hosmer's ambivalence about slavery and contains a reference to "Strange Fruit," a song made famous by Billie Holiday. The quotation in stanza 3 is from the Preface to Child's *An Appeal in Favor of That Class of Americans Called Africans* (Boston: Allen & Ticknor, 1833). The quotation in stanza 4 is from a letter Child wrote to Hosmer, September 16, 1860 (Carr 162).

"From Backyard Studio, to Rome, 1852": American actress Charlotte Cushman retired to Rome with her partner Matilda Hayes. Cushman was a supporter of Hosmer and invited her to live with them when she first went to Rome.

"Finding My Master": Hosmer's teacher, sculptor John Gibson, had been apprenticed to Antonio Canova.

"My First Child, and Another Daughter": Hosmer's words about grizzled locks are quoted from her letter to Mrs. Carr, January 1, 1858 (Carr 119).

"My First Full-Figure Daughter" contains lines from Tennyson's "Oenone."

"On Marriage, How Many Times Must I Tell You": Hosmer wrote to Wayman Crow from London in July, 1873 "With all my banging about I thrive like a green bay tree" (Carr 300).

"Rumor": Stanza 1, line 1, William Story (Sherwood 63); line 2, John Gibson (Carr 21); line 3, Lydia Maria Child (Sherwood 37); line 4, Frederic Leighton (Sherwood 71). Stanza 2, line 2, Elizabeth Barrett Browning (Sherwood 118); line 4, Henry James (Sherwood 321). Stanza 3, line 2, Maria Mitchell (Sherwood 162); line 4, Elizabeth Barrett Browning (Sherwood 91). Stanza 4, line 2, Elizabeth Barrett Browning (Sherwood 204); line 4, Robert Browning (Sherwood 307). Stanza 5, line 2, Thomas Crawford (Sherwood 107); line 4, *Boston Sunday Globe*, March 1, 1908 (Curran Vol. III, Watertown Public Library). In stanzas 4 and 5, Marian is Lady Marian Alford (Sherwood 204).

"Her Story, My Daughter Beatrice" contains lines from Shelley's "The Cenci: A Tragedy." Beatrice revises Shelley in the penultimate stanza: Shelley wrote, "The crimes which mortal tongue dare never name/ God therefore scruples to avenge."

"Beatrice Dreams" is inspired by Tennyson's "The Eagle." The epigraph quotes from Hosmer's letter to Miss Dundas, September 27, 1856 (Carr 77).

"Hatty's Anxiety Dream" refers to Hiram Powers, another American sculptor who moved to Rome.

"Purification" contains references to and a line from Keats's "Endymion"; in my imagining, Keats's illness reminds Hosmer of her mother's, and the burning of furniture from the consumptive's sickroom evokes her earlier decision to be cremated.

"My Clothes": The convent escapade is documented (Sherwood 160–161); the last line is from Marianne Moore's "The Pangolin."

"Hatty Revises Current Fashion" paraphrases parts of an undated, unsigned article (SL, Microfilm reels 1-3). The cast mentioned is *Clasped Hands of the Brownings.*

"Zenobia Speaks, in Chains and Free": My sense of this and other Hosmer figures was influenced by Joy S. Kasson's provocative *Marble Queens and Captives* (New Haven: Yale University Press, 1990).

"The Critics Comment on *Zenobia*" consists primarily of direct quotations. Stanzas 1 to 4 contain remarks from various sources (Kasson 155–158); stanza 5 is from Charles Sumner, 1864 (Carr 204); stanza 6 from an 1864 *Atlantic Monthly* article (Carr Appendix B 365); stanza 7 from a *Chicago Evening Journal* article of June 14, 1865 (Carr Appendix B 366); stanza 8 from a poem inspired by the statue of Zenobia (Kasson 160).

"Thomas Hart Benton, in Bronze" contains passages from Hosmer's acceptance letter (Carr Appendix A 362–363).

"Hatty to Posterity" declines to solve the matter of her sexuality, since it did not seem finally a problem to her. The physical description of Louisa is based on language in a letter from Lady Paget (Sherwood 265).

"My Rome, Vanishing": Several adjectives in the first two lines of stanza 2 are Hosmer's (Sherwood 319); lines 4 and 5 contain a view Hosmer expressed (Carr 334). The ideas of lines 4 and 5 in stanza 5 and lines 1 and 2 in stanza 8 are contained in Hosmer's letter to Mrs. Carr, October 30, 1854 (Carr 42).

"Hatty's Dream, 1902": Several landscape details appear in Hosmer's letter to Miss Dundas (Carr 74–75).

"I Didn't Want to Admit It" contains quotations from Hosmer's formula for artificial marble, which was patented but never produced (SL, Reel 8 1a–3a), from Frances Power Cobbe (Carr 336), and from Ruth A. Bradford's address to the Watertown Historical Society following Hosmer's death (SL, Carton 1, Folder 1, 5). The theories referred to are mentioned in more than one source, including an article by Martha Vicinus, "Laocoöning in Rome: Harriet Hosmer and romantic friendship" (*Women's Writing*, Vol. 10, No. 2, 2003), in which the author gives greatest credence to Hosmer as lesbian. Though not directly relevant to the poem, Henry Adams's thoughts on power suggest an intriguing historical perspective on Hosmer's combined pursuits of art and mechanics (*The Education of Henry Adams: An Autobiography*, Ch. XXV, "The Dynamo and the Virgin").

"The Tenth Muse": The first two lines are in Hosmer's handwriting beneath her sketch of the Brownings' clasped hands (SL, Photonumber A162-175f-1).

"February 21, Then and Now" contains language from Carr (43 and 61) and from Hosmer's letter to Wayman Crow of February, 1872 (SL, Box 1, 1–18). The cleaning instructions are part of an unprocessed collection, no date on the fragment in Hosmer's handwriting (SL, Box 1, 1–18). Hosmer is buried in Mt. Auburn Cemetery in Cambridge, Massachusetts.

A complete list of Hosmer's sculptures and their locations as of October 1975 appears in Father Joseph Curran's Hosmeriana at the Watertown Public Library, Watertown, Massachusetts.

Many of Hosmer's sculptures can be viewed on Harvard University Library's Visual Information Access website, *http://via.harvard.edu*.